Moon

WONDER STARTERS

Moon

Illustrated by Gordon Davies

Published by WONDER BOOKS
A Division of Grosset & Dunlap, Inc.
A Filmways Company

51 Madison Avenue   New York, N.Y. 10010

About Wonder Starters

Wonder Starters are vocabulary controlled information books for young children. More than ninety per cent of the words in the text will be in the reading vocabulary of the vast majority of young readers. Word and sentence length have also been carefully controlled.

Key new words associated with the topic of each book are repeated with picture explanations in the Starters dictionary at the end. The dictionary can also be used as an index for teaching children to look things up.

Teachers and experts have been consulted on the content and accuracy of the books.

Published in the United States by Wonder Books, a Division of Grosset & Dunlap, Inc.

Library of Congress Catalog Card Number: 76-50354
ISBN: 0-448-09693-5 (Trade Edition)
ISBN: 0-448-06451-0 (Library Edition)

First U.S. Printing 1977

© Macdonald and Company (Publishers),
Limited, 1971, London.

Printed and bound in the United States of America.

It is bedtime.
I can see the moon in the sky.
The moon is far away.

Here is a big moon rocket.
The rocket engines fire.
The moon rocket goes up into space.

2

There is a spacecraft on top of the rocket.
Three astronauts are in the spacecraft.

3

Now the astronauts are near the moon.
They have left the rocket behind.
Two astronauts will land on the moon.
They will land in the lunar module.

4

Now the astronauts are landing.
The other astronaut
stays in the command module.

The lunar module lands on the moon.
It lands near a crater.
There are many craters on the moon.

6

Now the astronauts are on the moon.
Their spacesuits keep them cool.
They can jump very easily.

There is no air on the moon.
The astronauts need air to breathe.
They keep air in their backpacks.

Plants and animals need air too.
They cannot grow on the moon.
Nothing grows on the moon.

There are stones and dust on the ground.
The men put some stones in a box.
10

They will take the stones back to earth.
They can see the earth from the moon.

Now the two astronauts leave the moon.
They are in the lunar module.
They meet the other astronaut.
He is in the command module.

The three men come back to earth
in the command module.
They leave the lunar module behind.

There is air all around the earth.
The command module gets very hot.
The air and speed make it hot.
14

Soon the parachutes open.
The command module
comes down slowly.
It splashes down in the sea.

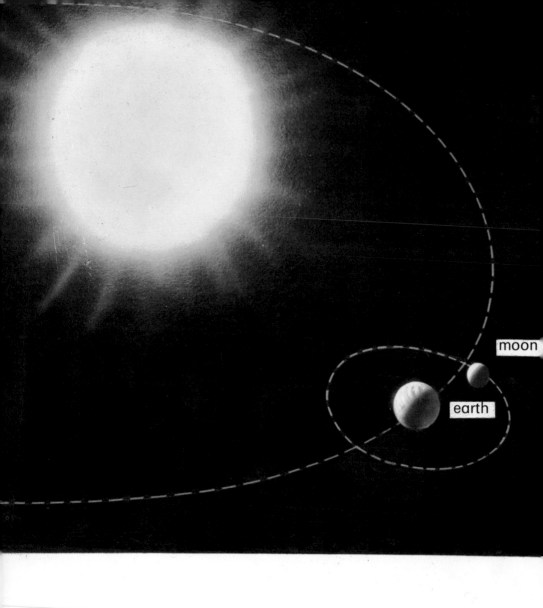

The sun shines on the earth.
The sun shines on the moon too.

16

You can see the sunny part of the moon.
You can see it best at night.
You cannot see the dark part
of the moon.

On some nights there is a full moon.
On other nights there is a half moon
or a quarter moon.

18

Long ago people did not know
what the moon was.
Some people said it was a man or a god.

Then people made telescopes.
You can see the moon better
with a telescope.
Here is one of the first telescopes.

This is one of the biggest telescopes
in the world.
It is in America.

See for yourself.

Look at the moon through binoculars.
Look for the craters on the moon.

Starter's **Moon** words

rocket
(page 2)

engine
(page 2)

spacecraft
(page 3)

astronaut
(page 3)

lunar module
(page 5)

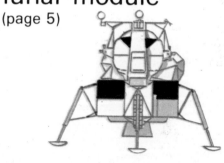

crater
(page 6)

backpack
(page 8)

earth
(page 11)

command module
(page 14)

parachute
(page 15)

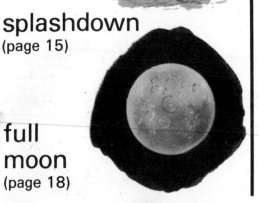

splashdown
(page 15)

full
moon
(page 18)

half moon
(page 18)

quarter
moon
(page 18)

telescope
(page 21)

binoculars
(page 22)